GARDEN JOU[RNAL]

_____

_____

_____

_____

_____

_____

_____

GARDEN JOURNAL

*There can be no other occupation like gardening in which,
if you were to creep up behind someone at their work, you
would find them smiling.*

Mirabel Osler

Use the following page to write a brief description of your garden and what it means to you. Note down areas you like and areas you think need improvement and the environment and feelings you want to create when you are walking through your garden.

garden journal

INSPIRATION

Come into the garden, Maud,
For the black bat, night, has flown,
Come into the garden, Maud,
I am here at the gate alone;
And the woodbine spices are wafted abroad,
And the musk of the rose is blown.

Alfred Lord Tennyson (1809–1892)
Maud; A Monodrama (excerpt from Part I)

Use the following pages make notes of the things that inspire you and influence you in your garden. Collect images and photographs of gardens that have elemnts and ideas that you like and would like to re-create in your own garden.

inspiration

inspiration

inspiration

inspiration

inspiration

inspiration

inspiration

inspiration

inspiration

PLANS AND IDEAS

I have never had so many good ideas day after day as when I worked in the garden.

John Erskine

PLANS AND IDEAS

*It is a golden maxim to cultivate the garden for the nose,
and the eyes will take care of themselves.*

Robert Louis Stevenson

Use the following pages to plan your garden ideas. There are graph pages to plot out your garden design and areas for lists of plants and supplies needed to create the effect you want to achieve and help you plan a budget for each project you undertake.

plans and ideas

plans and ideas

ITEM OR SERVICE					SUPPLIER AND COST

plans and ideas

ITEM OR SERVICE │ SUPPLIER AND COST

plans and ideas

ITEM OR SERVICE	SUPPLIER AND COST

plans and ideas

ITEM OR SERVICE	SUPPLIER AND COST

plans and ideas

ITEM OR SERVICE	SUPPLIER AND COST

SPRING

*It is utterly forbidden to be half-hearted about gardening.
You have got to love your garden whether you like it or not.*

W.C. Sellar and R.J. Yeatman, *Garden Rubbish*, 1936

SPRING

Spring, the sweet spring, is the year's pleasant king,
Then blooms each thing, then maids dance in a ring,
Cold doth not sting, the pretty birds do sing:
Cuckoo, jug-jug, pu-we, to-witta-woo!

Thomas Nashe (1567–1601)
Spring, the sweet spring (excerpt)

spring

TIPS FOR EARLY SPRING

- Lily of the valley love shade. Plant now or divide and replant if they are spreading in your garden from previous years. Their sprays of scented flowers are attractive in a corner of the garden during the spring.

- Snowdrops are like winter aconites – best moved and planted just after or during flowering to avoid roots drying out.

- Grow early flowering chrysanthemums now to plant outside in mid spring. Make sure soil is well prepared in advance.

- Many shrubs are grown for their attractive colours in winter; the bark of some brambles, dogwood and willows are especially striking. Prune them now to ensure brightly coloured new shoots. Any cut stems will root easily if large branches are pushed firmly into the soil.

- Clip winter flowering heathers with shears now to ensure their shape remains compact.

- Large shrubs can be successfully moved in autumn if preparation starts now. Trim the roots and encourage strong new fibrous roots to reduce the shock of repositioning later in the year.

spring

spring

SPRING TASK LIST

AREA	WORK TO BE DONE

spring

TIPS FOR MID SPRING

- Now is the time to plant annual climbers from seed.

  Cathedral bells, nasturtiums and morning glory can be planted in a sunny spot supported by a fence or pergola.

- Save money and time by buying plugs of bedding plants from a garden centre or seed catalogue now when they are ready for transplanting.

  Plant out when in flower in late spring after danger of frost is over.

  Clear up borders, cutting away dead growth, weeding and forking over soil.

  Remember to use compost not peat. A sprinkling of organic or rose fertiliser for new plants or those which are being moved is needed now.

- Divide sweet violets and move to a shady spot for the summer.

- Now is the time to start planting herbaceous borders with summer flowering plants

spring

spring

TIPS FOR LATE SPRING

- Towards the end of spring bedding plants need attention.

    Begonias, alyssum, petunias and salvias can go in to fill spaces and provide bright colour.

- Don't forget that annual delphiniums and tall asters will start flowering in early-mid summer. Together with annual nemesias you will have a wonderful display of colours, pink, white, yellow, crimson and blue.

- Tobacco plants, annual poppies in a range of yellows, white and orange and poor man's orchid will catch the eye.

- Don't miss annual pinks and new varieties of phlox.

    Plant out dormant dahlia tubers.

- They are tender plants which don't like even a hint of frost. Their flamboyant flowers will dazzle your garden later in the summer.

- Remember when choosing dahlias that they make wonderful cut flowers.

    Try to grow several rows of mixed types amongst the vegetables. Choose size and height carefully.

spring

spring

MY GARDEN IN SPRING

Use this area for photographs of your garden in Spring.

SUMMER

Weather means more when you have a garden. There's nothing like listening to a shower and thinking how it is soaking in around your green beans.

Marcelene Cox

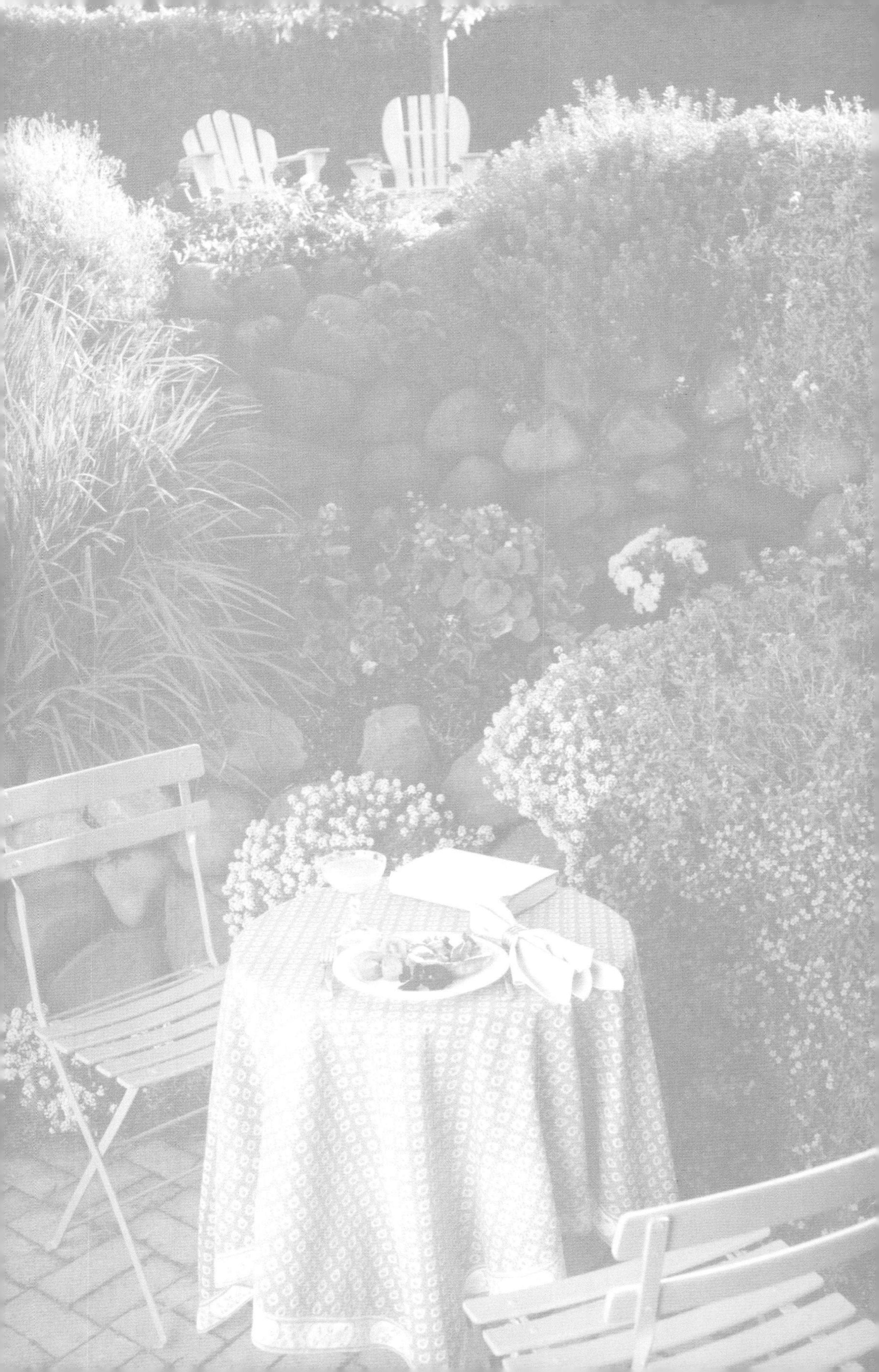

SUMMER

Now swarthy Summer, by rude health embrowned,
Precedence takes of rosy fingered Spring;
And laughing Joy, with wild flowers prank'd, and crown'd,
A wild and giddy thing,
And Health robust, from every care unbound,
Come on the zephyr's wing,
And cheer the toiling clown.

John Clare (1793–1864)
Summer Images (excerpt)

summer

TIPS FOR EARLY SUMMER

- Shade the greenhouse to exclude all hot sunshine during your absence. This helps to protect all your plants during the time you are away.

- Forget-me-nots can be pulled up after flowering.

- Wallflowers, sweet william and Iceland poppies can be sown in pots or in the garden.

- Cover pansy seeds with seed compost and keep cool and dark. Check regularly – seedlings emerge in about two weeks. Plant outside or transfer to modules and grow on till mid autumn. Colourful winter pansies are popular and give pleasure right through until spring.

- This is the time to ensure you work hard to train climbing roses. Try to get thorny branches where you want them and tie them well in. Sweet pea rings are useful for this and can be handled even with gloves on.

- Warmer weather brings out garden pests to attack the contents of your vegetable garden at this time. Watch out for cabbage root fly and carrot fly. It is important to take precautions when you plant – a piece of old carpet will protect cabbages; carrots can be hidden amongst onions – the strong smell confuses the flies.

- Watch out for fruit pests which disappear seconds after they have laid their eggs. There are various traps which will cut the problem drastically and protect your fruit crops.

- Prepare for short supplies of water by installing a rainwater butt.

summer

summer

TIPS FOR MID SUMMER

- Irises are good flowers for a wide range of colours, which make a wonderful show in the garden each year. They are easy plants to grow and demand a well drained, dry sunny spot. Make sure you have dug in manure or compost before planting. Divide these plants every 3 or 4 years about five weeks after flowering ends.

- Cut down early flowering herbaceous perennials now to avoid self seeding and future over-crowding.

- Lift daffodils and split into individual bulbs. Dry off and store in a cool place to replant in autumn.

- Soft tip cuttings of herbaceous perennials and shrubs can be taken now. They will root fast in high temperatures. Lavender especially benefits from replacement regularly every few years.

- In a hot dry summer lawns will begin to suffer noticeably. Mow less frequently and leave the grass quite high. Allow cuttings to stay on the lawn for a thin mulch. Give an extra feed in autumn just before rain.

summer

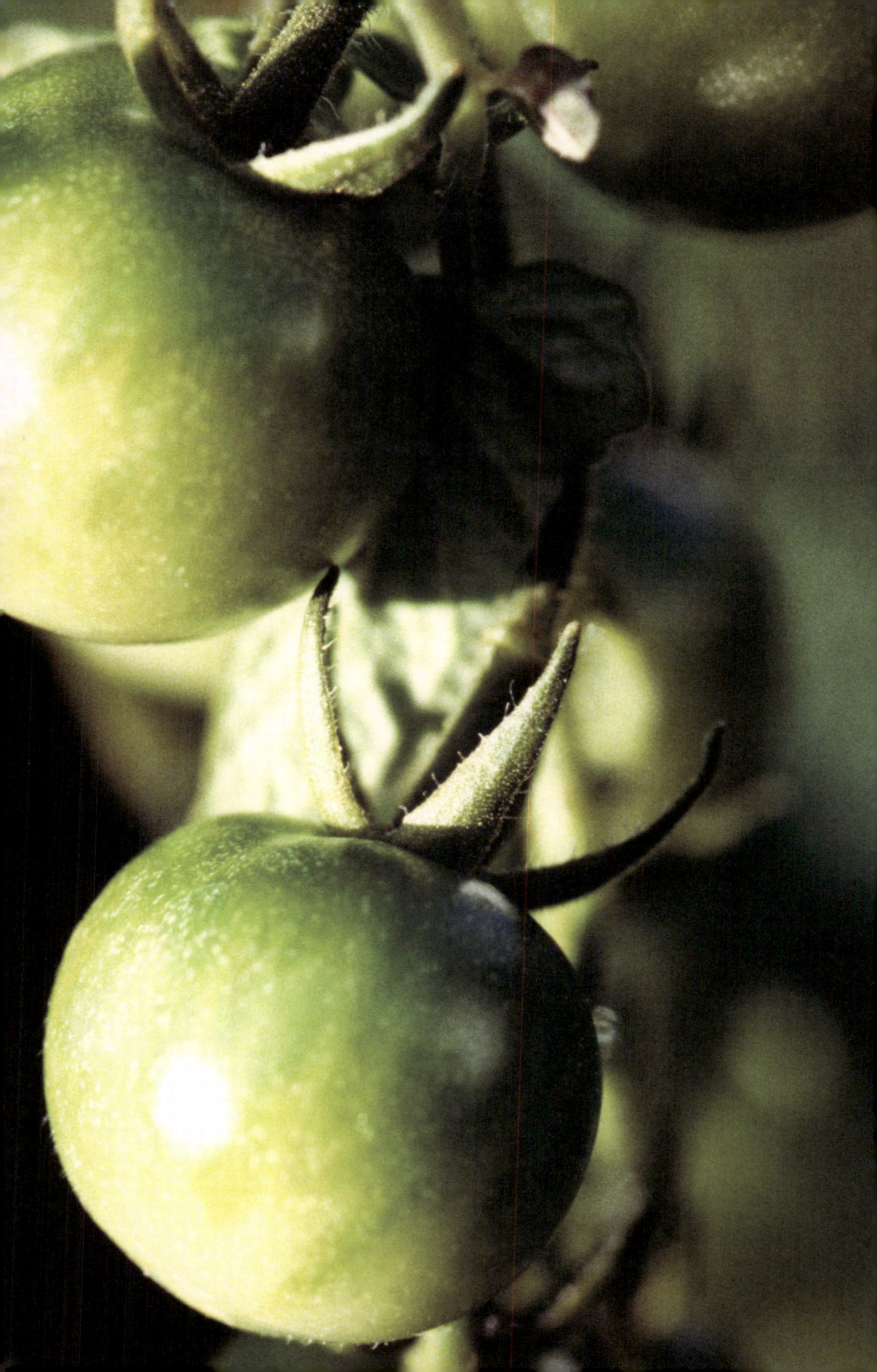

summer

SUMMER TASK LIST

AREA					WORK TO BE DONE

summer

TIPS FOR LATE SUMMER

- Plant autumn flowering bulbs in late summer. Think ahead and order them from a reputable mail order supplier early in the season.

- Try to use up seeds from spring sowing to rejuvenate containers at this time. A late batch of flowers provides a welcome splash of colour.

- Summer prune any vigorous climbers and shrubs now. Wisteria should be pruned in late summer – reduce side-shoots to 3–5 leaves. Rambling roses will also need attention at this time.

- Now is the time to buy new strawberry plants. There are many varieties which can be grown in sequence to provide good crops throughout the season. Begin planning for next year.

- This is a good time to turf a lawn or prepare to sow lawn seed. A well tended lawn enclosed by well packed borders provides a welcome oasis in any size garden.

summer

summer

MY GARDEN IN SUMMER

Use this area for photographs of your garden in Summer.

AUTUMN

The best place to seek God is in a garden.
You can dig for him there.

George Bernard Shaw, *The Adventures of the Black Girl in Her Search for God*, 1932

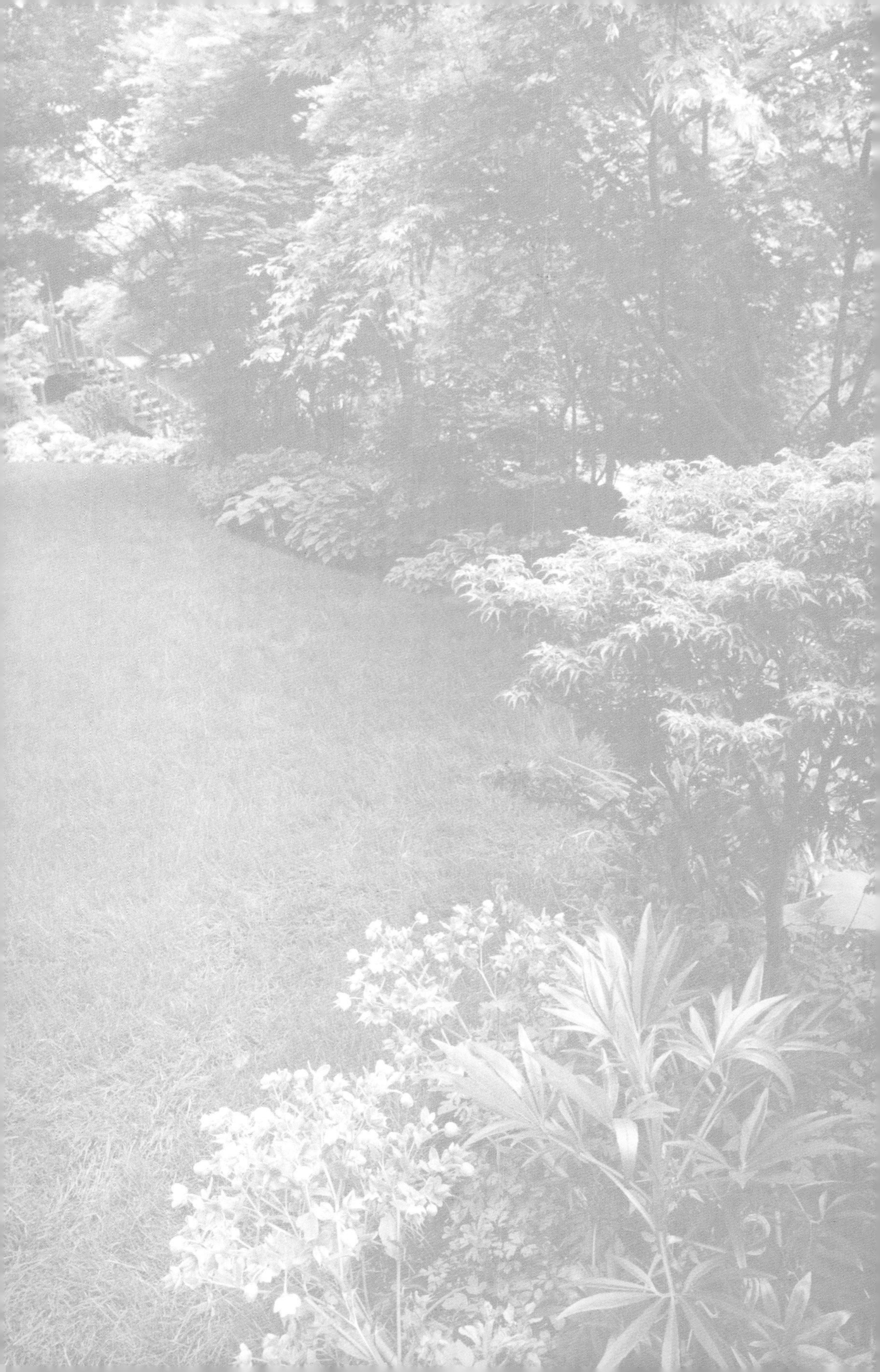

AUTUMN

Good-bye, good-bye to Summer!
For Summer's nearly done;
The garden smiling faintly,
Cool breezes in the sun;
Our Thrushes now are silent,
Our Swallows flown away, –
But Robin's here, in coat of brown,
With ruddy breast-knot gay.
Robin, Robin Redbreast,
O Robin dear!
Robin singing sweetly
In the falling of the year.

William Allingham (1824–1889) *Robin Redbreast* (excerpt)

autumn

TIPS FOR EARLY AUTUMN

- Leave dahlias outside until the first threat of frost.

    Lift tubers and shake off soil.
    Trim off old stems.
    Put tubers upside down for a week to drain then pack in cardboard boxes – right way up, to store in cool place.

- Work manure or garden compost into soil to revive it after the summer.

- Collect seeds from the garden – the cheapest way to produce lots of new plants for next year. Many hardy perennials can be sown as soon as they have been dried and will germinate quickly now or in the spring.

- A wide range of bulbs available now will provide a bright garden next spring. Start with daffodils which could flower for a hundred days; the earliest variety start in late winter and end with those which finish flowering in late spring. Plant at the right depth.

- Pumpkins, marrows and all winter squash vegetables must be well seasoned before storing. Cut when they are a good colour and have reached full size. Lie them in the sunshine for two weeks or so to harden. A greenhouse or sunny windowsill will protect them from the wet.

- Remember the benefits of a greenhouse. It should repay its' initial cost in about two years. This is a good time to start thinking about buying one. Your choice of greenhouse will depend on your budget. You will get what you pay for and usually it is sensible to buy the best you can afford.

autumn

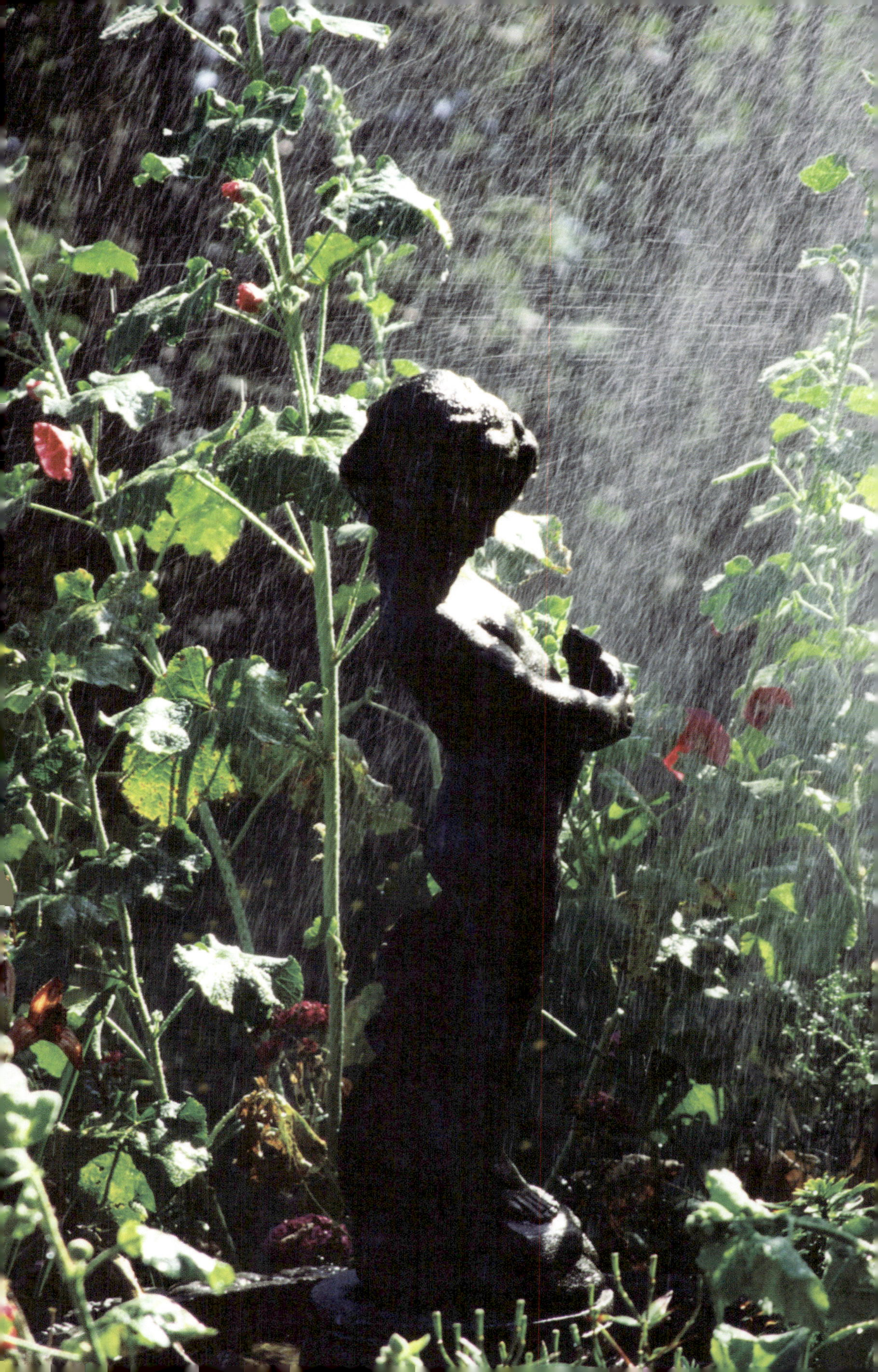

autumn

AUTUMN TASK LIST

AREA   WORK TO BE DONE

autumn

TIPS FOR MID AUTUMN

- For winter containers choose wood, clay or stone for extra protection from frost.

    Before frosts arrive wrap your pots with sacking or bubble polythene to avoid your plants freezing.

- Plant pots for winter. Begin by ensuring good drainage and use good compost on top. Bulbs will give early colour; evergreens in the centre provide height. Choose good bushy plants and remember that winter pansies, wallflowers and forget-me-nots will give extra variety.

- You could plant a boundary hedge now to ensure privacy from neighbours in the future. In a windy spot a hedge makes an excellent windbreak. In small gardens take care that your hedge does not take up too much precious space. Look at both deciduous and coniferous hedges and perhaps mix them.

- Lift and store root crops now. A few vegetables can be left in the ground – celeriac, parsnips and salsify gain flavour after a touch of frost.

- Garlic which has been exposed to two or three months of cold weather early on is best planted now. Try to buy seed bulbs and prepare a sunny spot to develop fat bulbs for next summer.

autumn

autumn

TIPS FOR LATE AUTUMN

- Prepare to plant late flowering tulips in the first half of winter after all other spring bulbs.

    They need a light soil and a sunny spot; try to avoid mixed borders.

- Bare-rooted roses can be bought now and will be better than container grown plants. The best time for planting is when they have lost their leaves.

- It is more expensive to lay a lawn with turf than to grow from seed. If you prefer the instant finish, make sure you buy the best turves you can which are guaranteed weed free. This is the best time of the year to lay turf but delay if the ground is very wet or frozen.

- Only water if the weather is exceptionally dry.

- The dark strong leaves of winter leeks improve their flavour after frost.

    They can be lifted and stored in compost in a shed to last through several months.

- Plant new apple and pear trees now. Carefully assess the amount of space available in your garden before making your final choice. There are several varieties of frost tolerant apples and pears which will be happy in colder regions.

- Your greenhouse will retain more warmth if it is insulated. Bubble polythene can be fixed inside the glass. Keep the greenhouse well ventilated on mild days – a small crack of air for about an hour will help keep disease at bay. Protect container plants carefully.

autumn

autumn

MY GARDEN IN AUTUMN

Use this area for photographs of your garden in Autumn.

WINTER

Nature does not complete things. She is chaotic. Man must finish, and he does so by making a garden and building a wall.

Robert Frost (1874 - 1963) US poet

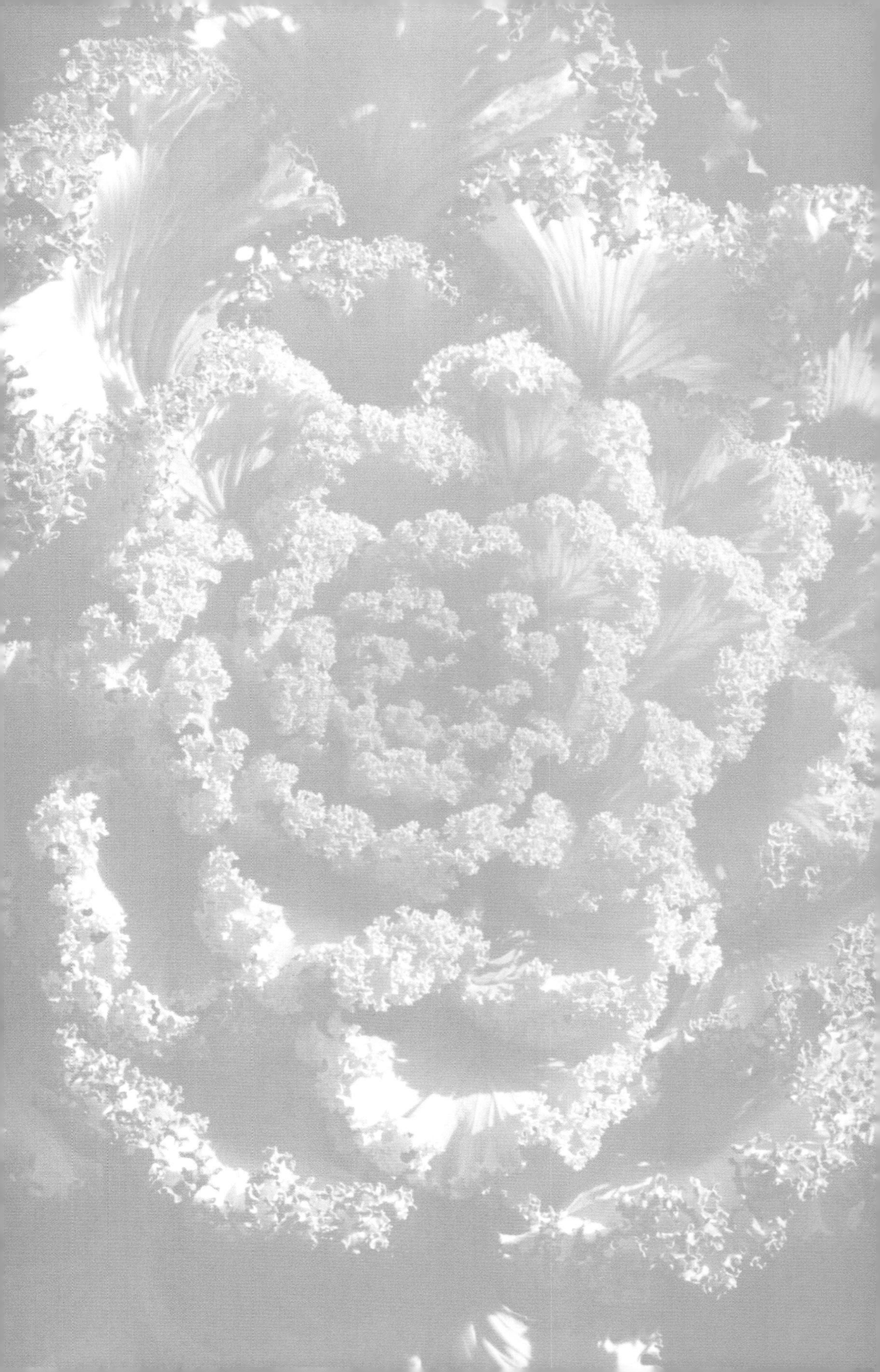

WINTER

Blow, blow, thou winter wind,
Thou art not so unkind
As man's ingratitude.
Thy tooth is not so keen,
Because thou art not seen,
Although thy breath be rude.
Hey-ho, sing hey-ho, unto the green holly.
Most friendship is feigning, most loving, mere folly.

William Shakespeare (1564–1616) from *As You Like It*, II.7

winter

TIPS FOR EARLY WINTER

- You can grow pelargoniums from seed and this is the right time.

    Use a propagator because the seeds need a temperature of at least 65°F to germinate.

- When the leaves of deciduous trees have fallen they can be pruned and shaped. Small gardens may benefit from reducing the overall size and branches can be thinned.

    Hard pruning promotes new growth.

- Prevent wind damage to long stemmed roses, shrubs and climbers this month by cutting back or tying in.

- On the days when the sun does shine go and check the vegetable garden.

- After a hard frost make sure that any new plants have not lifted. If necessary firm them down.

winter

winter

TIPS FOR MID WINTER

- Order deep frozen runners from specialist suppliers for spring delivery. When planted the sudden change in temperature means that they can crop in only 60 days after planting.

- Young plants and cuttings in the greenhouse benefit from the gentle warmth of a heated mat trapped under a polythene cover. Heating a whole greenhouse at this time of year is too expensive many plants can be raised indoors on windowsills or in the airing cupboard.

- Lawns which squelch underfoot need spiking to remedy poor drainage.

- Start to think about vegetables to harvest later in the season; make first sowings indoors. Prepare soil for later planting.

    Cover area set aside for first plantings with thick polythene sheeting or cloches to keep bed dry and warm.

    On windowsills or in the greenhouse start sowing seeds for plants to be ready to go outside from late winter.

- Sow small quantities – early cabbage, cauliflower and lettuce which do not need high temperatures and germinate at 55°F.

    When big enough prick them out to 5cm and grow on in light.

- Start early potatoes; order seed potatoes now in time for preparation before planting out in spring. Sprout or chit to advance first harvest and increase crop size.

winter

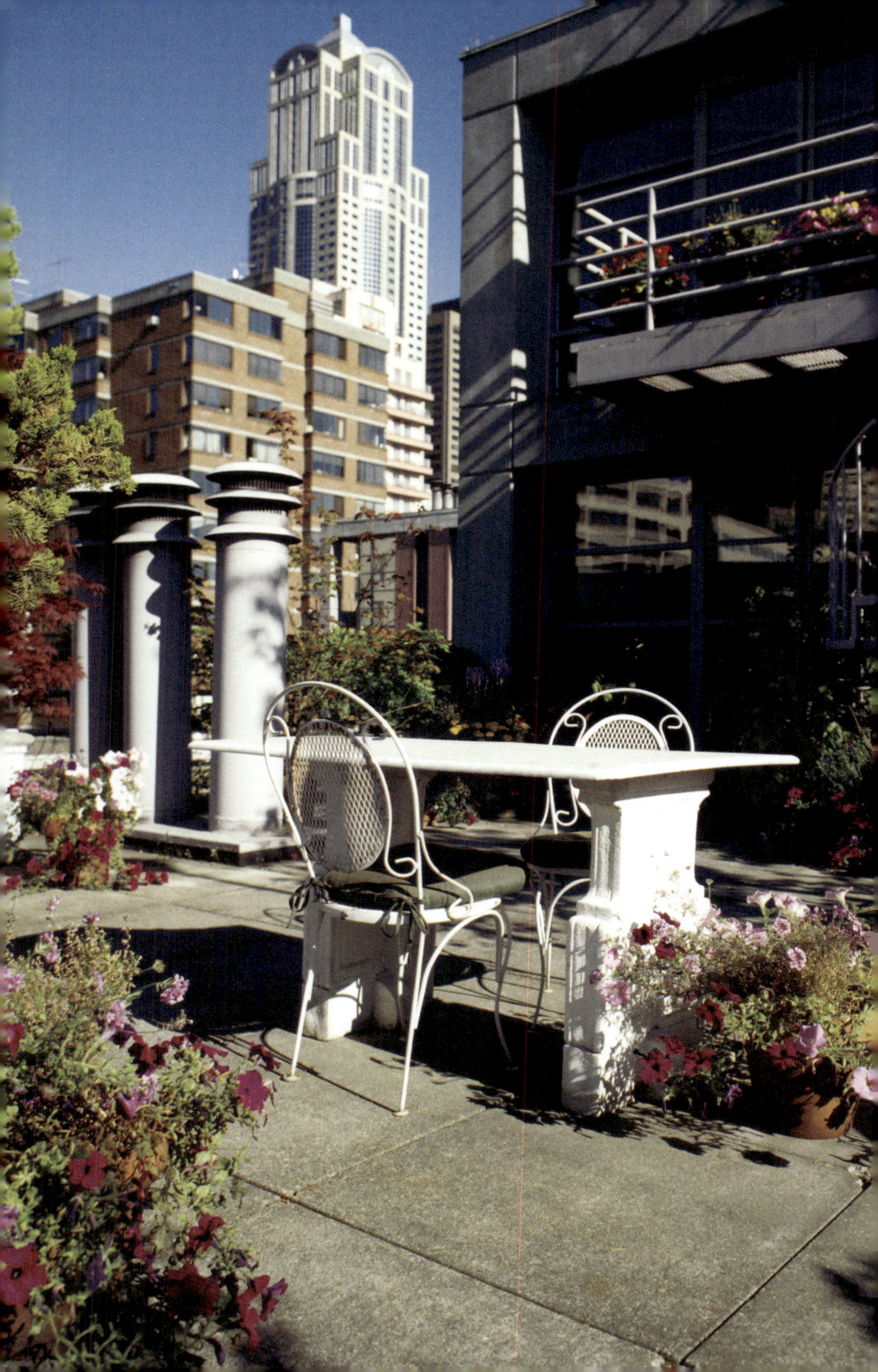

winter

WINTER TASK LIST

AREA	WORK TO BE DONE

winter

TIPS FOR LATE WINTER

- Look after seedlings. Keep an eye on your seedlings as they begin to come up – they need plenty of light. If they are indoors make sure they are on the windowsill.

- Make a light box for seedlings.

    Cut the front out of a large cardboard box.

    Paint the inside white – this forms a reflector.

    line the base with foil and use this to ensure your seedlings get plenty of light without being scorched by sun or killed by cold.

- Put your light box on a table by the sunniest window – be prepared to give your seedlings the protection of a sheet of newspaper when necessary.

- Bring out your stored dahlias and other perennials now. The boxes of compost in which they have spent the winter should be topped up and they need a little water. Spray them occasionally – it helps to stimulate the growth of the strongest shoots.

- Bring any potted spring bulbs indoors to force them. Put them on a sunny windowsill in a cool room till flower buds colour – then bring them into a warmer room to enjoy them.

- Now is the time to begin planning sowing of tomatoes in the greenhouse. Choose a variety well known for flavour. Sow seeds in gentle heat and transplant to pots when a full pair of seed leaves appear. In mid spring they will be ready to plant out in the greenhouse.

winter

winter

MY GARDEN IN WINTER

Use this area for photographs of your garden in Winter.

NOTES AND CLIPPINGS

You can bury a lot of troubles digging in the dirt.

Anon

NOTES AND CLIPPINGS

*Our England is a garden, and such gardens are not made
By singing: "Oh, how beautiful!" and sitting in the shade.*

Rudyard Kipling, *The Glory of the Garden*

Use the following pages to note down any tips you have been given by other gardeners or any useful clippings you find in magazines or newspapers.

notes and clippings

notes and clippings

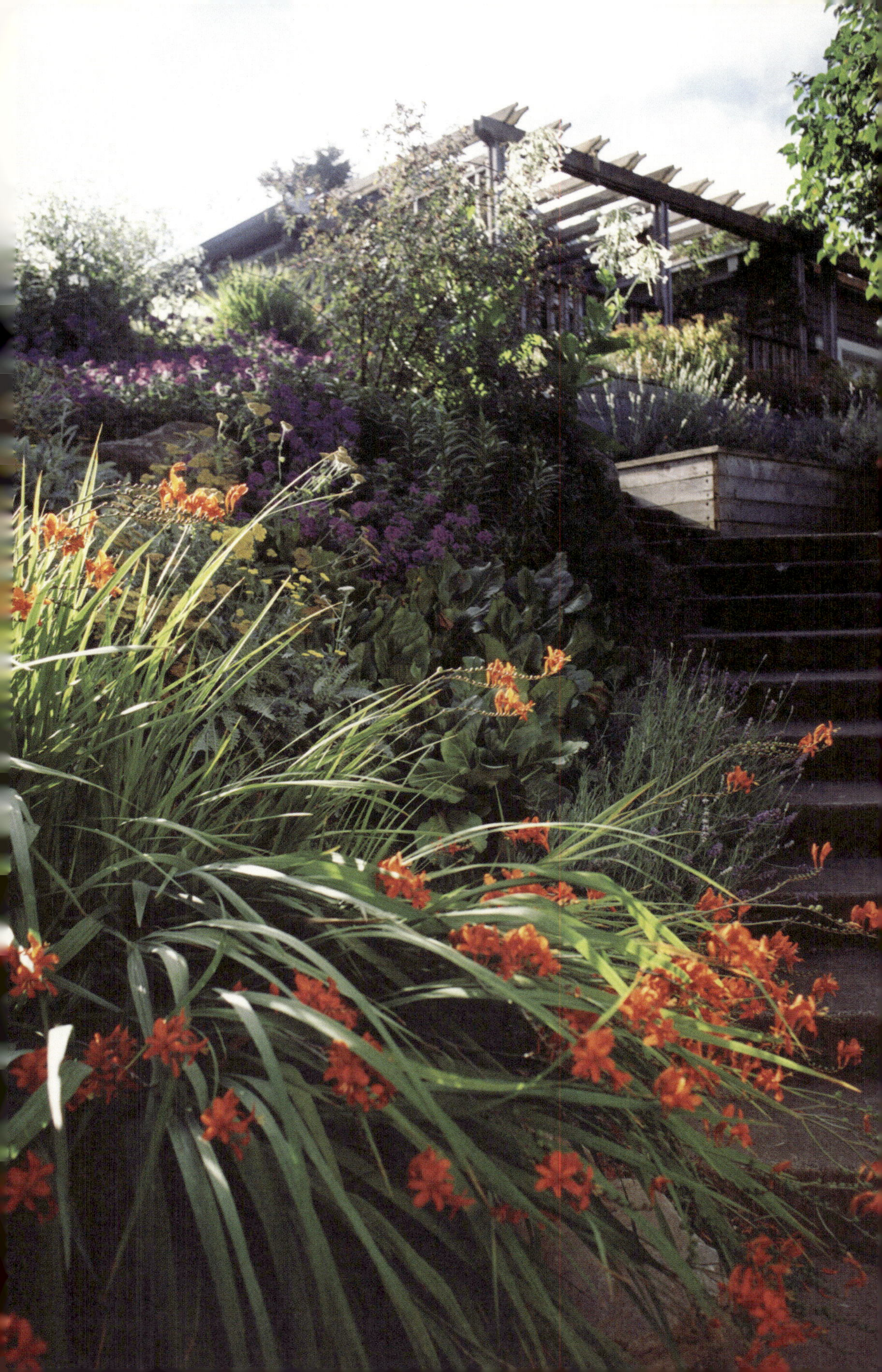

notes and clippings

notes and clippings

notes and clippings

notes and clippings

notes and clippings

notes and clippings

notes and clippings

notes and clippings

USEFUL CONTACTS

One of the healthiest ways to gamble is with a spade and a package of garden seeds.

Dan Bennett

USEFUL CONTACTS

Many things grow in the garden that were never sown there.

Thomas Fuller, *Gnomologia*, 1732

useful contacts

CONTACT DETAILS   NOTES

name

address

telephone

mobile

fax

email

www

name

address

telephone

mobile

fax

email

www

name

address

telephone

mobile

fax

email

www

useful contacts

CONTACT DETAILS   NOTES

name

address

telephone

mobile

fax

email

www

name

address

telephone

mobile

fax

email

www

name

address

telephone

mobile

fax

email

www

useful contacts

CONTACT DETAILS					NOTES

name

address

telephone

mobile

fax

email

www

name

address

telephone

mobile

fax

email

www

name

address

telephone

mobile

fax

email

www

useful contacts

CONTACT DETAILS									NOTES

name

address

telephone

mobile

fax

email

www

name

address

telephone

mobile

fax

email

www

name

address

telephone

mobile

fax

email

www

useful contacts

CONTACT DETAILS NOTES

name

address

telephone

mobile

fax

email

www

name

address

telephone

mobile

fax

email

www

name

address

telephone

mobile

fax

email

www

useful contacts

CONTACT DETAILS					NOTES

name

address

telephone

mobile

fax

email

www

name

address

telephone

mobile

fax

email

www

name

address

telephone

mobile

fax

email

www

PULTENEY PRESS

Published in 2008 by Pulteney Press,
1 Riverside Court, St John's Road, Bath BA2 6PD

Designed and produced for Pulteney Press
by Open Door Limited, Rutland UK

© copyright this edition 2008, Pulteney Press ltd
© copyright design 2008, Open Door ltd

Images: © Photodisc Inc. Getty Images

All rights reserved. No part of this publication may be reproduced, stored in a retrieval system or transmitted in any form or by any means, electronic, mechanical, photocopying or otherwise, without the prior permission of the copyright owners.

ISBN: 978 1906734152